Cardinal Numbers

An Ohio Counting Book

Written by Marcia Schonberg and Illustrated by Bruce Langton

Sleeping Bear Press
310 North Main Street
P.O. Box 20
Chelsea, MI 48118
www.sleepingbearpress.com

Printed and bound in China.

10 9 8 7 6 5 4 3 2 1

Library of Congress Cataloging-in-Publication Data
Schonberg, Marcia.
Cardinal numbers : an Ohio counting book / author, Marcia Schonberg ;
illustrator, Bruce Langton.
p. cm.
Summary: Presents short rhymes about numbers of objects from one through fourteen
and provides information about the Ohio natural history and social studies topics that
the objects represent. Also includes a set of open-ended counting problems.
ISBN 1-58536-084-8
1. Counting-Juvenile literature. 2. Ohio-Description and travel-Juvenile literature.
[1. Counting. 2. Ohio.] I. Langton, Bruce, ill. II. Title.
QA113 .S387 2002
[E]—dc21
2002007344

Cardinal Numbers *is about the numbers we find in Ohio
and ones we use each day. Special thanks to educators Lisa Shambaugh,
Karen Higgins, and Grace Sunbury for their professional suggestions.
They dedicate themselves to making teaching and learning a personal,
creative, and meaningful experience—like the ones you can gather
along with the buckeyes within these pages.*

To Brandon and Joel whose smiles bring me countless amounts of joy each day.

To Bill who's always been "Number 1" to me.

M.S.

*This book is dedicated to all the wonderful children that
have touched my heart throughout my life.*

*To Rebecca, Brett, and Rory... Without you my life would not be the same.
Thank you for just being there.*

*Lastly, my thanks to Sleeping Bear Press and Marcia Schonberg for
all their hard work and dedication on such a wonderful book.*

B.L.

There are tiny buckeyes
hiding in our book.
Maybe 1 on every page.
Take a careful look.

1 plump blimp
hanging in the sky.
Wouldn't it be fun
to ride so very high?

A blimp is an airship that is shaped like an egg, but much larger in size. Unlike a hot air balloon, a blimp is dirigible, meaning it can be steered.

The *Spirit of Goodyear* blimp flies above special events in Ohio and across the U.S. Spectacular camera views from the blimp are transmitted to television control trucks on the ground. It advertises Goodyear tires, but is also used to raise money for charity. The blimp flies to disaster sites and helps the Red Cross give messages to those below. Blimps cruise at an average speed of 35 miles per hour.

When the *Spirit of Goodyear* is not flying, it docks at the Akron Airship Base in Sheffield. It measures 192 feet long, 55 feet in diameter, and 59.5 feet high. It has 202,700 cubic feet of volume. There are 2 more Goodyear Blimps in the U.S.: the *Eagle* in California and the *Stars and Stripes* based in Florida.

1

Ohio immigrants began building canals to connect Lake Erie with the Ohio River. The first segment of the Ohio and Erie Canal was completed between Cleveland and Akron in 1827. It took 7 years to dig the entire 309-mile-long canal by hand. Workers made sure the canals were 4 feet deep and wide enough for 2 boats traveling in opposite directions to pass. Locks raised and lowered the water level to maintain the depth. Approximately 1,000 miles of canals were built in Ohio between 1825 and 1847.

Teams of mules or workhorses followed the towpath, a narrow trail along side the canal, as they pulled the boats. Many of these old paths are popular multiuse bikeways today.

Canal boats traveled 2 to 4 miles an hour. The cost for a boat trip varied depending on the distance traveled, but passengers usually paid 2 to 5 cents per mile to travel on a canal boat.

Before fast cars and trains
canal boats were fun to ride.
Slowly, they were towed
by 2 horses, side by side.

The white trillium is Ohio's state wildflower. It has 3 petals, 3 sepals, and 3 leaves. The white trillium turns pink as it gets older. Wildflowers first appear in early spring when the daylight increases and there is more sunlight. The southwestern part of Ohio sees the first blooms in early April. There are 2,300 species of wildflowers in Ohio.

3

Count the petals,
1, 2, 3.
Now count white trillium.
How many do you see?

Can you find the Canada goose
guarding the river's shore?
Then find fluffy yellow goslings
lined up in rows of 4.

Canada geese migrate to Ohio, but Giant Canada geese live here year-round. They mate for life. That is why the gander helps the female protect their young goslings each spring. Identify Canada geese by the white patches that look like chin straps below their short bills. Listen for their distinctive honks. Look for their V-shape during flight. You will see them in Ohio's lakes and streams.

Ohio has more than 60,000 miles of streams. An average of 38 inches of water from rain, ice, hail, and snow feed Ohio streams every year. Streams in the northern third of Ohio flow into Lake Erie. From Lake Erie the water flows into the Atlantic Ocean by way of Lake Ontario and the St. Lawrence Seaway.

Streams more than 100 miles long are called rivers. The Muskingum, Scioto, and Great Miami are just a few of the rivers that flow south to their final destination in the Gulf of Mexico.

Paddling **5** canoes,
    beneath the summer sun.
On Ohio's rivers,
    what could be more fun?

Ohio's rivers are fun places and there's no better way to explore them than by canoe. Put on a life jacket and learn how to paddle a canoe. You can travel along many streams including the 11 special river systems that are part of the Ohio State Scenic Rivers System.

Streams in Ohio are home to fish and many other forms of life. If you go fishing, the first thing you must learn is to have patience. While you are waiting for a fish, look for dragonflies as they dart above the water or go below. There are many species of turtles and snakes living in Ohio streams too. Listen for bullfrogs that say *jug-o-rum*, *jug-o-rum* and green frogs that call out a *twang* sound. Maybe you will see a salamander, an amphibian with a tail.

5

The black racer snake was named the state reptile in 1995 because racers are found in each of Ohio's 88 counties. This snake eats small rodents such as mice so farmers consider it a friend. Its scientific name is *Coluber constrictor*, but it is not a constrictor. There are 2 kinds of racer snakes in Ohio, the black racer and the blue racer. They are called *racer* because they can move up to speeds of 8-10 miles per hour. The largest snake in Ohio is the black rat snake. It can grow to 8 feet in length.

Racer snakes are predators. Because they eat mice and rats, racers help farmers control the rodent population. About 46 different species and subspecies of snakes make their home in Ohio's natural areas.

6

6 black racer snakes
hiding near the barn.
They may slither and surprise you,
but they are helpers on the farm.

GENERAL STORE

Drive down country roads,
looking all around.
Count 7 Amish buggies,
hitched in an Amish town.

Amish and Mennonite people love the land and like to farm, but they also enjoy creating beautiful hand-made quilts and furniture. Most of them immigrated from Switzerland searching for religious freedom. They were called Anabaptists. Ohio's counties of Holmes, Wayne, Tuscarawas, and Stark have the greatest Amish population (about 35,000) in the world. Some also live in Geauga County.

The Amish do not drive automobiles or use electricity. Businesses in Amish communities have hitching posts for horse and buggies, and parking lots for non-Amish drivers. Do you know one way to tell if a farmhouse is Amish? You won't see any electrical wires or telephone poles. They believe in living simply without modern conveniences, but they have fun and enjoy themselves like everyone else. It is against their religious teachings to be photo-graphed so please respect their wishes when you visit.

Ohio is 1 of 7 states to name the cardinal as its official state bird. It is the most popular of all state birds and became Ohio's favorite in 1933. The cardinal does not migrate—it stays all winter. It munches sunflower seeds at backyard feeders. It also eats other seeds, berries, and insects. Both the male and female have a crest (a tuft of feathers atop their head), long tail, and red bill, but the male is the beautiful bright red bird we easily identify. The feathers on a female and young cardinal are camouflage colors of light brown.

8

Bright red cardinals
bring us to number 8.
Look very closely.
Can you match each with a mate?

9 Longaberger baskets
handmade in many shapes.
Filled with Ohio foods—
tomatoes, corn, and grapes.

Visitors come from all over the U.S. to see the world's largest basket in Dresden. It is woven from strips of maple and measures 48 feet long. In the Longaberger factories, artisans weave more baskets than anywhere else in the United States.

Half of Ohio's land is considered prime farmland. Only 3 other states have such high percentages of fertile land as Ohio. Farmers in Ohio grow food for people all over the world. They put Ohio in the top 10 for harvesting tomatoes, corn, and grapes as well as other farm products like soybeans, oats, and wheat.

In 1912, when candy maker Clarence Crane created the first Life Saver, mint was the only flavor.

Mr. Crane owned a candy shop in Cleveland. His chocolate candy melted during the hot summer. He knew that most mints imported from Europe were square and individually wrapped and they didn't melt easily. The idea for the round candies came to him one day when he was at the pharmacy. There he saw a pill maker, a device used for making small round pills by hand. He used it to create a round shape and then punched a tiny hole in the middle of each circle. The tiny round shapes reminded him of the life preservers used on ships so he called them Life Savers. He invented them in his hometown of Garrettsville. Today, Life Savers come in 25 flavors.

Shiny round Life Savers
are such fun to eat.
Line them up and count to **10**
before you taste your treat.

11 hikers in the woods
walking 1 by 1.
  Explore the Buckeye Trail—
wouldn't that be fun?

BUCKEYE TRAIL

The Buckeye Trail is the longest hiking trail in Ohio. It leads hikers 1,250 miles around the perimeter of the state. Portions of the trail connect to existing roads while other parts follow the towpath of the Ohio-Erie Canal and old railroad beds. You will see forests, parks, and cities if you hike the entire trail. The route is marked by light blue rectangles about 2 X 6 inches in size. These blue blazes guide you along the trail.

There are many other paths to hike in Ohio too. Find one that winds around lakes, streams, or old canal locks, or hike a trail that has hills and valleys. You may even know a trail that follows city streets. Where is your favorite hiking spot?

11

Sugar shack is the term for the building where maple sap is boiled into syrup. Ohio has 800 sugar shacks, some operated by large companies and others by individuals.

Ohio usually produces more maple syrup than any other state except Vermont, New York, and sometimes Pennsylvania. The amount of syrup Ohio produces depends on the weather. The ideal weather for harvesting sap is warm, sunny days followed by cold evenings. It takes 40 gallons of sap to make 1 gallon of syrup. Maple trees are used to collect sap because they are plentiful in the northeast U.S. and have a high concentration of sugar.

Long ago, Native Americans filled hollowed-out logs with sap and added heated rocks to make syrup. Early pioneers cooked their sap outdoors in black pots over an open flame. Today, modern maple syrup producers use evaporators. These devices make 1 to 2 gallons of maple syrup in an hour.

12

Now we have 12 buckets
collecting maple sap.
We'll make sweet syrup
up at the sugar shack.

What hangs on Ohio's state tree
       hiding in a prickly shell?
Find **13** round buckeyes
       Ohioans know so well.

The Ohio buckeye tree has been the official state tree since 1953, but its roots and name go back centuries. Native Americans named the shiny brown nut "hetuck," meaning the eye of a buck or male deer. Pioneers chose buckeye wood for the base logs of their cabins. They believed it resisted insects. Later, William Henry Harrison used the buckeye tree as a symbol during his presidential campaign in 1840.

Today, the state champion buckeye tree grows in North Bend near Cincinnati on land once owned by John Aston Warder, the founding father of the American Forestry Association. While most Ohio buckeye trees grow to 30-50 feet tall, the state champion is 82 feet high and measures 162 inches in circumference. The leafy branches can spread out to 67 feet wide.

It takes 3 days to make 1 whistle at the American Whistle Corporation in Columbus. This small factory makes more than 1 million whistles a year and is the only manufacturer of metal whistles in the United States. The whistles made here are the loudest in the world. Police departments, community organizations, schools, the National Football League (NFL), and youth soccer associations purchase them.

Whistles are made of different types of metals from chrome and brass to 24-karat gold plate. People who work outdoors in winter buy rubber Safe-T-Tips for their whistles to keep their lips from sticking to the cold metal.

14

14 shiny metal whistles
make the shrillest sound.
In a game or traffic jam,
a whistle can be found.

Author's note: The following problems reflect a creative and open-ended approach to mathematics. Answers, while not always specific, encourage discussion, divergent thinking and dialogue among children and between children and adults.

Classroom teachers across the grade levels and state encouraged me as I created the remaining pages. They serve as a starting point—one that, hopefully, will lead to the wonderment of self-discovery. Please use any of the numbers and topics in *Cardinal Numbers* to help your child acquire number concepts while learning about themselves and the state of Ohio.

Most of all, I hope you have as much fun sharing these "buckeye" numbers as I had in writing them.

—M.S.

We've counted Ohio numbers,
starting with number 1.
Now use your imagination.
It's time to have more fun.

You'll find clues in these pages
and sometimes answers, too.
But discovering possibilities
is what we each must do.

Problem 1:

The size of the Goodyear blimp
is 192 feet.
Is it bigger than your room?
Or a house on your street?

Problem 2:

Arrange 192
in groups that are smaller.
100s, 10s and 1s.
Now, isn't that much easier?

Buckeye nuts are not always brown and shiny. The nut is white before it ripens. Folklore says that half of the nut is poisonous and that squirrels know which half is safe to eat. More likely, the nut is so bitter that squirrels stop before the whole nut is eaten.

Problem 3:

Picking up buckeyes
1 handful at a time.
Can you hold 2, 4, or 6?
Now, how many can you find?

Problem 4:

How wide is a buckeye?
   Measure it to see.
     If you make a buckeye necklace,
      how long will it be?

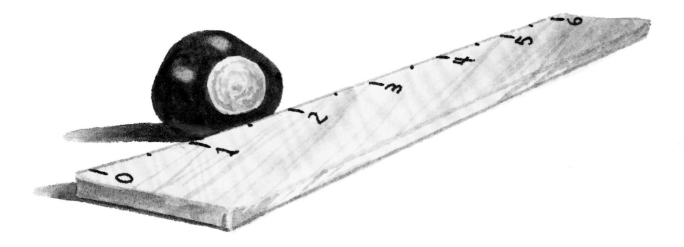

Here are rural counting facts
to learn what farmers grow.
Ohio farms lead the world.
Just do the work below.

Problem 5:

Swiss cheese cut in yellow cubes.
How many do we have?
Please count them all.
Now count just half.

Problem 6:

Dad bought a dozen eggs
    for his hungry family of 4.
        Each person ate 3 scrambled eggs.
           Could anyone have more?

Ohio produces more Swiss cheese than any other state.

Ohio chickens lay a lot of eggs. In 2001, Ohio cluckers produced 7.9 billion eggs, making it the second largest egg producer in the country. Ohio is second because Iowa has more chickens.

Ohio ranks number 1 in the variety of apples grown in the U.S. Some well-known Ohio apples are Golden Delicious, Red Delicious, Jonathon, Melrose, and Stayman. Specialty varieties like Fuji, Gala, and Granny Smith are increasing in popularity, but are not as plentiful as others. Which apple is your favorite?

Problem 7:

Mmm. Mom's making apple crisp.
Count the apples she will need.
Is the pan round or square?
How many kids will she feed?

Problem 8:

Sweet syrup with breakfast.
How much do you pour?
How many servings in a gallon?
When will you need more?

Ohio is the 7th most populated state of all 50. Can you make a fraction that explains this fact?

It is 205 miles wide and 230 miles long at its farthest points. It has 88 counties. The largest county is Ashtabula in the northeast corner of the state. Right next to it is Lake County, our smallest. The highest point in Ohio is at Campbell Hill, near Bellefontaine. At 1,550 feet above sea level, it is the highest spot between the Appalachian Mountains and the Mississippi River. The lowest point in Ohio is along the Ohio River, near Cincinnati, at 455 feet above sea level.

Problem 9:

Ohio is just 1 state—
    there are 50 in all.
  We think our state is big
    until we make a fraction and then it seems so small.

Problem 10:

How large is Ohio? (44,828 square miles)

      How many people live in our state? (11,353,140 in 2000)

    Now use your calculator—

       how many people per square mile does that make?

We've learned our numbers.
Found many buckeyes too.
Ohio has more math to do,
but now it's up to you—because our book's all through.

Marcia Schonberg

Ohio native and award-winning journalist Marcia Schonberg is a frequent contributor to the *Columbus Dispatch* and a variety of national publications. Her articles and travel guides also appear on the worldwide web. She is the author of Ohio travel guides. Marcia is an active member of the Ohioana Library Association, American Society of Journalists and Authors, Midwest Travel Writers Association, and the Society of Children's Book Writers and Illustrators. She lives with her husband, Bill, in Lexington, Ohio.

Bruce Langton

Bruce Langton is considered a premier contemporary artist. His unmistakable style and unique ability to capture not only sporting and wildlife scenes, but also landscapes has won him numerous national awards and international recognition. Bruce travels nationwide to make interactive presentations to schools and libraries about illustrating children's books.

With over one hundred limited edition prints and etchings on the market, Bruce is now proud to add children's books to his list of achievements: *B is for Buckeye: An Ohio Alphabet, V is for Volunteer: A Tennessee Alphabet, H is for Hoosier: An Indiana Alphabet,* and *Cardinal Numbers: An Ohio Counting Book.* Bruce resides in Indiana with his wife Rebecca and two sons, Brett and Rory. He enjoys spending time teaching Kyokushinkai karate and teaming as a professional clown with his son Rory.